Fiona Macdonald

OXFORD
UNIVERSITY PRESS

is a department of the University of Oxford.
It furthers the University's objective of excellence in research, scholarship, and education by publishing worldwide in

Oxford New York
Auckland Cape Town Dar es Salaam Hong Kong Karachi
Kuala Lumpur Madrid Melbourne Mexico City Nairobi
New Delhi Shanghai Taipei Toronto

With offices in

Argentina Austria Brazil Chile Czech Republic France Greece
Guatemala Hungary Italy Japan Poland Portugal Singapore
South Korea Switzerland Thailand Turkey Ukraine Vietnam

First published 2007

British Library Cataloguing in Publication Data

Data available

ISBN: 978-0-19-846122-7

9 10

Printed in China

Paper used in the production of this book is a natural, recyclable product made from wood grown in sustainable forests. The manufacturing process conforms to the environmental regulations of the country of origin

Acknowledgements

The publisher would like to thank the following for permission to reproduce photographs: **p7** Visual Arts Library (London)/Alamy; **p8**l Erich Lessing/AKG – Images, **p8**r Archaeological Museum Beirut/Dagli Orti/Art Archive; **p10** Ullstein – Rîhrbein/AKG – Images; **p11**t Kojan & Krogvold/Museum of Cultural History – University of Oslo, Norway, **p11**b Norsk Folkemuseum; **p12**bl Visual Arts Library (London)/Alamy, **p12**br Musée Rolin Autun France/Dagli Orti/Art Archive, **p12**t Museum of London/HIP/TopFoto; **p13** Private Collection/Dagli Orti/Art Archive; **p14** Paul Russell/Weald & Downland Open Air Museum; **p15**t Archives CDA/Guillot/AKG – Images, **p15**c Victoria & Albert Museum, **p15**b Universal Pictorial Press Photo/TopFoto; **p16** National Maritime Museum, London; **p17**bl Capt. Roald Amundsen/Royal Geographical Society, **p17**br TopFoto, **p17**t Mike Greenlar/The Image Works/TopFoto; **p18**t J Marshall/Tribaleye Images/Alamy, **p18**b Marcus Wilson-Smith/Alamy; **p19**t TopFoto, **p19**b Liu Liqun/Chinastock; **p20**l The Print Collector/Alamy, **p20**r Mary Evans Picture Library; **p21** A.H. Beard Pty Ltd.; **p22** Corbis UK Ltd.; **p23**t TopFoto, **p23**b William Hart/Stone/Getty Images

Cover photograph: Corbis

Illustrations by Maurizio de Angelis/Beehive Illustration: **p6**b, **p21**; Mike Lacey/Beehive Illustration: **p6**t, **p7**, **p9**, **p16**, **p22**, **p23**; Sean Longcroft: **p4**, **p5**

Contents

What does your bedroom look like?

Beds are very important! We spend one-third of our lives asleep in them. We read in bed, write, think – and dream. We bounce on our beds when we are excited and lie quietly in them when we feel ill.

Bedrooms are also special places. We keep our clothes and books there and our favourite toys. We can be private and secret in a bedroom, or play there with our friends.

But – at different times and at different places – beds and bedrooms have not all been the same. This book will show you some of them. How would you like to ...

...snore in straw on the floor?
ZZZ
...hide behind curtains?
...rock and roll in a cradle?
...hop into a hammock?
ZZZZ
...feel snug in a rug?
...rest on hard horsehair?
...burrow into a bunk?

Inside caves

The first-ever places specially made for sleeping were shelters of bones, skins, twigs and leaves. **Prehistoric** people built these in the open air and also inside caves. They made the world's first beds by digging sleeping-pits in the ground.

Sleeping pits for adults were about 90 cm long and 60 cm wide.

Q: Why do you think the sleeping pits were so small?

A: Because cave people slept curled up, on their sides. It was warmer that way.

Remains of a sleeping pit from Texas, USA, made around 8,500 years ago.

On the roof

In Ancient Egypt, families made beds on the flat roofs of their houses.

Around 3000 BC, the first raised beds were invented. They had four wooden legs with a wooden frame on top. The frame was covered with a pad of dried grass, or had ropes stretched across it. Raised beds were airy and comfortable to sleep on.

This golden bed was buried in boy-king Tutankhamen's tomb in Egypt around 1352 BC.

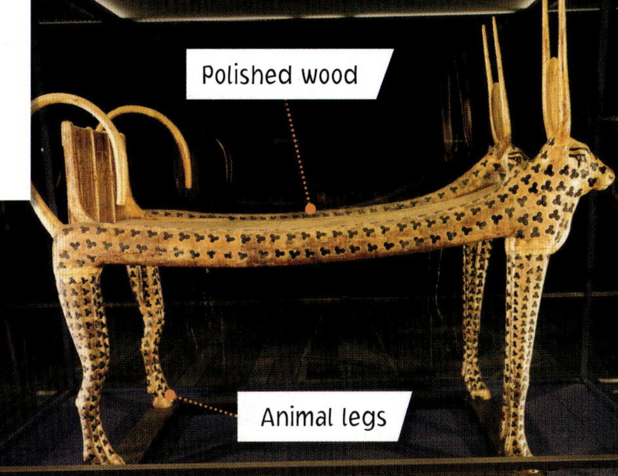

Quiz

Q: Why was it safe to put beds on roofs in Egypt?

A: Because it hardly ever rained there, so sleepers did not get wet.

Couches

The Ancient Greeks and Romans also had raised beds to sleep on. The best were richly carved, and decorated with painted patterns. But they also used their beds for sitting on during the day, while eating and drinking. At mealtimes, Greek and Roman diners lay on one side, propped up on cushions. They ate from little low tables in front of them.

Greek men reclining (leaning back) to enjoy music after a meal, around 490 BC.

This carving shows a Roman lady reclining on a couch. It was made about AD 200.

Fact Box

Beds used for sitting on or eating from are often called day-beds, or couches.

Rich and poor

In Ancient Greece and Rome, eating and sleeping arrangements were different for rich and poor families. Rich people's houses had several rooms. Some were public; visitors could enter. Some were private, and only for family use. Poor people usually lived, ate and slept in just one room.

How to go to bed ...

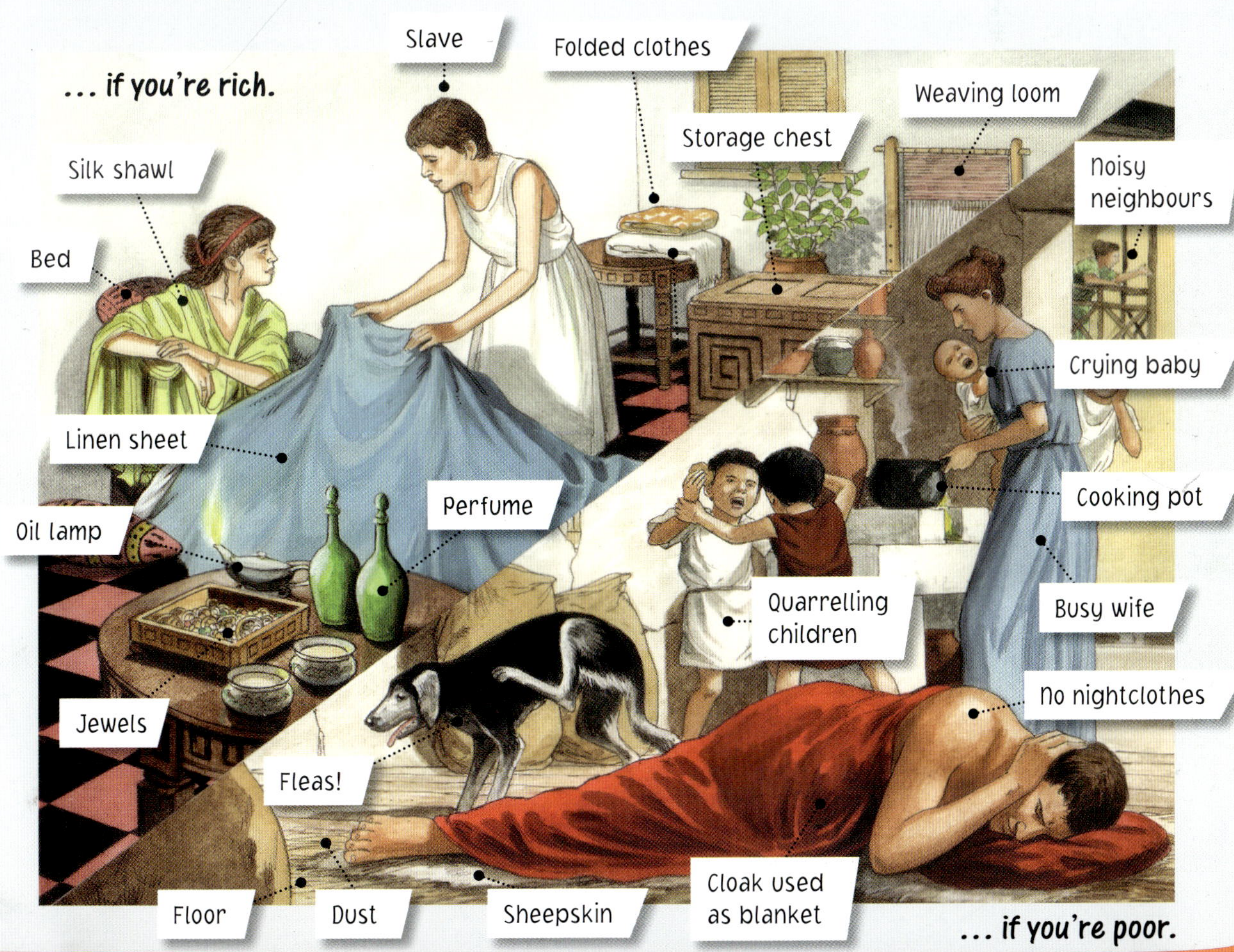

Beside the fire

It was cold in Viking lands. So **Vikings** built homes with big halls (living rooms) where whole families, their servants, warriors and guests could all eat and sleep close to a cosy fire. Most Viking halls had a table, some benches and some storage chests, all made of wood. But Viking beds were just low platforms of earth with straw mattresses, or heaps of furs, woollen rugs and feather quilts spread out on the ground.

A museum display, showing what a Viking home was like.

Saxon warriors settle down to sleep

After the feast, they pushed the benches away from the table ... and padded the floor with mats and pillows ... the glorious warriors laid their bright battle-shields by their heads, and stowed weapons and armour on the benches above them.

Adapted from **Beowulf**

Beds and screens

The richest, most powerful Viking people slept in decorated beds made of wood.

Other rich people chose to sleep behind wooden screens at one end of the hall. They set a fashion for hidden beds in warm living rooms. Hidden beds were built for hundreds of years.

A bed buried with a Viking princess in Norway, around AD 850.

A hidden cupboard-bed from a house in Norway, where the Vikings used to live. It was built around AD 1700.

Rock-a-bye, lullaby

Mothers tried many ways of keeping their babies safe from harm. They tied them to their backs in cloth slings, carried them in straw baskets, or wrapped them tightly in swaddling (strips of cloth). From around AD 1000, in Europe, mothers put babies in wooden rocking cradles. These stopped babies rolling off big beds or crawling on dirty, draughty floors. They also helped them sleep peacefully.

This wooden cradle on legs was made around AD 1500. Just a gentle push makes it rock backwards and forwards.

A baby wrapped in a shawl, around AD 1400.

Lullaby, from around AD 1400

Lullabies are soothing songs. They are also called 'cradle songs'. This one has a rocking rhythm, like a cradle.

'Lullay my liking,
My dear son, my sweeting.
Lullay, my dear heart,
My own dear darling.'
(my liking = someone I like)

A stone statue from Italy of a baby in swaddling, from around AD 1500.

Bedrooms – a new invention!

Before AD 1200, few houses in Europe had rooms set aside for sleeping. But lords and ladies in big castles wanted somewhere to get away from rowdy soldiers, noisy builders, busy servants, muddy farmhands and smelly dogs. They built solars (sunny, cosy, bed-sitting rooms), where they could relax peacefully. Other people soon copied them.

Fact Box

If lords and ladies owned several castles, they often took their favourite bed with them when they went to visit each one.

This shows a fifteenth century French bedroom.

Big window lets in air and sunshine

Bedside cupboard

Carved stone fireplace

Bench with cushions

Patterned tiles on the floor

Curtains keep out draughts

Candle holder hung from ceiling

Thick, warm bedspread

Bed is raised above ground

Quiz

Q: What was built next to solars?

A: Garderobes – little lavatories! Medieval people hung their best robes there. They thought the smell kept clothes-moths away. Today's word 'wardrobe' was originally 'garderobe'.

Four-posters

After AD 1500, rich Europeans built fine **stately homes** instead of castles. These looked grand, but were cold and draughty and needed lots of servants to run them.

For warmth and privacy, house-owners had four-poster beds with thick curtains. Four-posters had deep mattresses stuffed with wool or feathers, fancy covers and big pillows. Inside the curtains, rich people could be warm, comfortable, and alone. But they still needed servants to look after them. So they added truckle-beds where servants could sleep – down at floor level, outside the curtains!

Four-poster beds were very expensive, so they became status symbols. Kings and queens even sat on special state (government) beds to greet important visitors.

Bed curtains also cost a lot of money, and took many years to finish. They were made of fabric woven with patterns, or **embroidered** by expert craft workers or rich ladies.

The four-poster bed of King Louis XIII of France, around AD 1640.

These bed-curtains were hand-stitched in England by Abigail Pett, around AD 1680. We know little about Abigail's life, but we can still admire her skill.

Britain's biggest bed?

The Great Bed of Ware is probably the biggest bed ever made in Britain. A four-poster, it was built of oak by Jonas Forbrooke around AD 1590. It measures 3.33 metres long and 3.33 metres wide, and has room for 15 sleepers, side by side.

North and South America, from c. 5000 BC

Hammocks and sleeping bags

The beds people made depended on where they lived. Each bed had to suit the local environment, so that people could sleep in comfort and safety. Beds also had to be made from local materials. It was too difficult and expensive to bring materials from far away.

In tropical rainforests, biting insects and poisonous snakes crawled on the ground, and big cats prowled at night. So rainforest people twisted rope from plants, wove it into hammocks, and slung them high up between trees.

Hammocks were invented by Caribbean people. Columbus was the first European to see them.

Hammocks on an eighteenth century ship.

Borrowed bed words

The word 'hammock' came to Europe from the Caribbean. Explorer Christopher Columbus learned it from the Taino people who lived there, around AD 1500.

A Taino hammock used about 1.5 kilometres of cord, and took 13 hours to make.

In cold, snowy regions, people made bedding from the skins of caribou (reindeer) and Arctic hare. Reindeer hairs were hollow, and trapped air inside for **insulation**. Hare fur was soft and cosy. Arctic peoples also invented sleeping bags, to surround sleepers with warmth all night long.

Little sleeping bags were tied to wooden frames, called cradleboards, to carry babies safely. This photo shows an Algonquin baby from Canada in a traditional cradleboard.

A photo from 1907 showing Inuit people inside an igloo, resting on caribou skins.

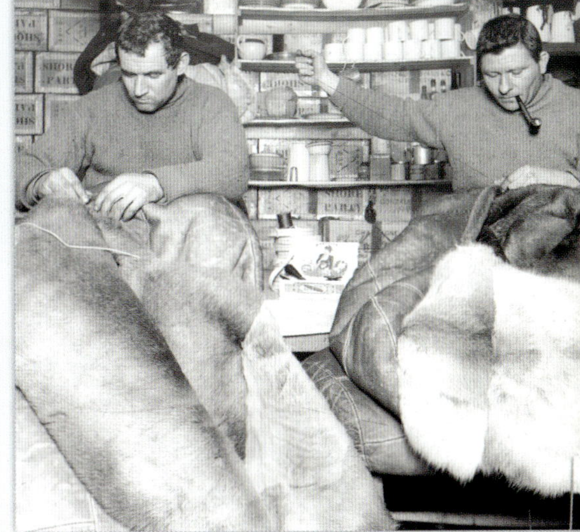

Sailors on Scott's Antarctic expedition, 1911, sewing sleeping bags.

Asia, from *c.* 3000 BC, or earlier

Rugs, mats and heated floors

In Central Asia, many people lived as **nomads**. They travelled to find grass to feed their sheep, goats and horses. They lived in yurts or gers (big tents), and slept on thick, warm rugs woven from bright coloured wool. On travelling days, the rugs were easy to roll up and carry.

Kilim (flat-weave) rug, woven in Turkey.

Rugs cover the floor and walls of this ger from Mongolia.

In Japan, houses were built of wood. Inside, there were moveable walls, made of wood and paper. Beds were moveable, too. Japanese families spread tatami (dried grass mats) on the floor, then added futons (pads filled with cotton wadding). In the morning, they folded up the futons and put them away.

A photo from 1890 showing a Japanese futon spread on a floor.

Screen

Futon

Tatami

This room in northern Shaanxi Province, China, has a kang with a baby sleeping on it!

In north China, houses were built of brick. To keep warm in winter, families built a kang (big, hollow, brick bench) to sit and sleep on. Hot smoke from fires used to cook evening meals flowed through pipes to the kang. Once heated, the kang stayed warm all night.

Quiz

Q: Why were Japanese walls made of paper?

A: So they would not kill people when they fell down. Japan has many earthquakes, so its houses were designed to collapse safely.

Brass bedsteads and bouncy springs

Around AD 1800, new industries developed in Europe and North America. New, steam-powered machines made all kinds of useful things very cheaply and quickly. For the first time, beds were mass-produced (made in large numbers), mostly from metal. The favourite metal for making beds was shiny yellow brass.

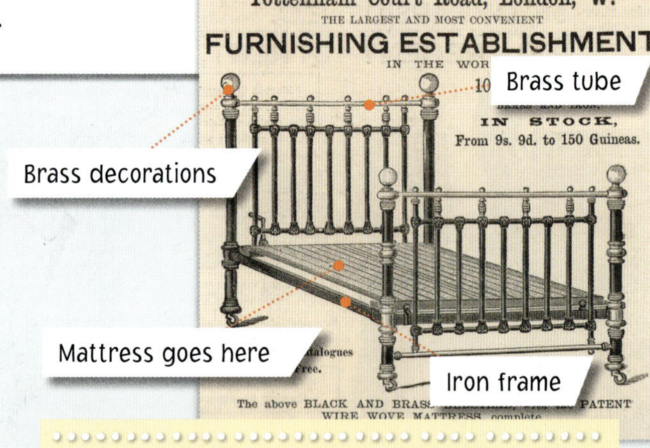

A brass bedstead, made in 1892. Factory workers said that brass beds were 'cheaper, cleaner and more elegant' than old-fashioned wooden ones.

Metal to make beds was produced in **foundries**, by heating crushed ore (rock that contains metal).

Hot work!

Brass is an alloy (mixed metal) made by melting two other metals, copper and zinc, together. The mixture needs to get very hot – around 1000 °C.

Around AD 1850, European metalworkers also discovered how to make springs from coiled steel wire. Spring mattresses, padded with horsehair, soon replaced wool and feather ones. They lasted longer, and people said they were cleaner and healthier. They were also less likely to contain bed-bugs, lice and fleas!

New bed-making industries soon spread worldwide. This lorry loaded with spring mattresses was photographed in Australia in 1933.

Springs for support

Springs make mattresses bouncy. There are two main kinds: open coil springs (pictured right) and pocket springs.

All the open coil springs (about 300) in a mattress are linked together. But each pocket spring is separate, and wrapped in a pocket (tube) of strong cloth.

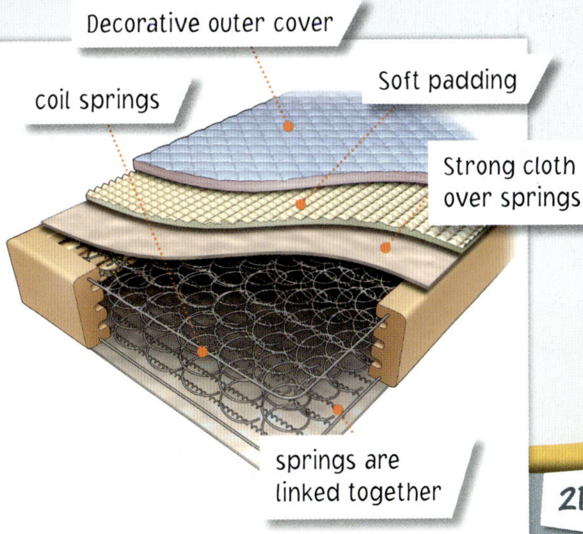

Bunks – old and new

Beds have changed a lot over the years. But a few bed designs have stayed the same. We still sleep in one old-style type of bed today – bunks!

The Romans invented bunks, around 2,000 years ago. They were built for soldiers in forts guarding the Roman Empire. From around AD 1750 to 1950, bunks were also built for European soldiers fighting in wars far away from home.

American soldiers in bunks in a battleship during the Second World War (1939–1945).

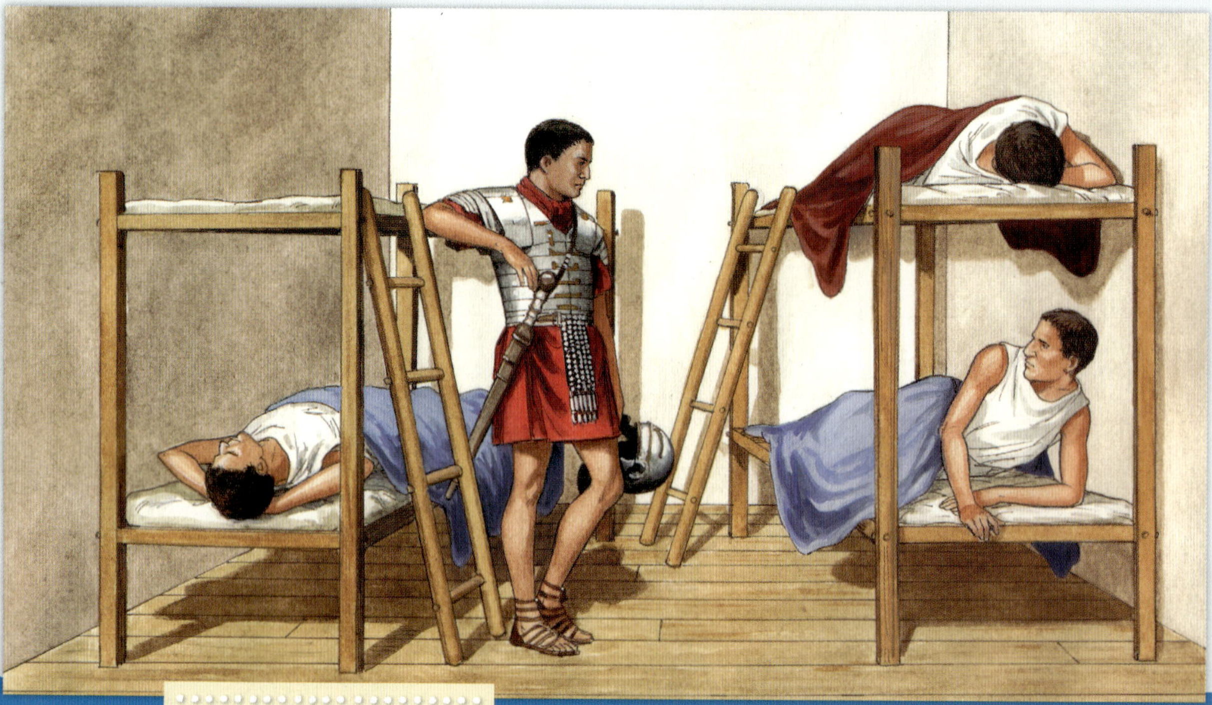

Bunks at a Roman fort.

Bunks were also built below decks on ships, to fit in as many sailors – or passengers – as possible. From around AD 1850, poor **migrants** travelling to America or Australia were crammed into tight bunks for long, miserable voyages.

During the Second World War Londoners had to sleep in underground shelters to protect them from bombs and rockets.

In the 20th century, special kinds of bunks were built for safety in wartime. Soldiers hid from enemies in dug-outs (bunks in underground trenches). Families left their homes to sleep on bunks in air-raid shelters.

But today, most bunks are fun!

My Perfect Bedroom

If you could design a perfect bedroom, what would it look like?

- Where would you build your bedroom?
- How would you decorate it?
- How would you make it cosy and comfortable?
- What would your bed be made of?
- What shape, size and colour would it be?
- How would it help you to relax and sleep well?
- What covers would you choose to keep you warm?

Glossary

Beowulf – Anglo-Saxon poem, written around AD 800. It tells the story of Beowulf, a hero, and the monster Grendel.

embroidery – cloth decorated with stitches in coloured thread.

foundry – factory or workshop where metal is melted and poured into moulds to make useful objects or works of art.

insulation – covering that stops heat, cold or electricity from passing in or out.

migrant – person who travels to settle in another country.

nomads – people who move from place to place to find pasture for their sheep, goats or cattle.

prehistoric – belonging to a time long ago, before written records were kept.

Saxons – people from north Germany. Saxon families settled in England around AD 500.

stately home – large and splendid house, usually belonging to a noble family.

Vikings – traders and pirates from Norway, Denmark and Sweden. They attacked northern Europe and settled there from around AD 800 to AD 1100.

Index